EMMANUEL JOSEPH

Curious Hearts, Exploring Nostalgia, Solitude, and the Resilience of the Human Soul

Copyright © 2025 by Emmanuel Joseph

All rights reserved. No part of this publication may be reproduced, stored or transmitted in any form or by any means, electronic, mechanical, photocopying, recording, scanning, or otherwise without written permission from the publisher. It is illegal to copy this book, post it to a website, or distribute it by any other means without permission.

First edition

This book was professionally typeset on Reedsy.
Find out more at reedsy.com

Contents

1	Chapter 1: Whispers of the Past	1
2	Chapter 2: Solitude's Embrace	2
3	Chapter 3: Resilient Souls	3
4	Chapter 4: Echoes of Childhood	4
5	Chapter 5: The Dance of Solitude and Connection	6
6	Chapter 6: Windows to the Soul	8
7	Chapter 7: The Art of Letting Go	10
8	Chapter 8: The Power of Vulnerability	12
9	Chapter 9: The Gift of Presence	14
10	Chapter 10: The Journey of Self-Discovery	16
11	Chapter 11: Finding Beauty in Imperfection	18
12	Chapter 12: The Strength of Vulnerability	20
13	Chapter 13: The Power of Forgiveness	22
14	Chapter 14: The Quest for Meaning	24
15	Chapter 15: Embracing Change	26
16	Chapter 16: The Language of Silence	28
17	Chapter 17: The Resilience of Love	30

1

Chapter 1: Whispers of the Past

Nostalgia is a strange and potent force, whispering sweetly of days gone by. It creeps into the quiet moments, painting the mind with sepia-toned memories. The scent of freshly baked bread, the sound of a familiar song, these small triggers transport us to a time where everything seemed simpler. It's a comforting embrace, reminding us of a time when our worries were fewer and our dreams boundless.

Yet, nostalgia is not without its thorns. It can trap us in the past, creating a longing for what can never be again. It's a delicate dance between cherishing the past and yearning for it. Each memory is a double-edged sword, bringing both joy and a pang of sorrow. But through this, we learn the art of balance, finding strength in memories while living in the present.

In this intricate tapestry of time, we find solace in the repetition of rituals that anchor us to our roots. These moments, small yet significant, are like stars in the night sky, guiding us through the present with echoes of the past. As we grow older, we realize that nostalgia is not a longing for a perfect past, but an appreciation for the journey that brought us here.

As the chapters of our lives unfold, we come to understand that the past is a part of our identity. It shapes us, influences our decisions, and molds our perspectives. By embracing nostalgia, we learn to appreciate the beauty of impermanence and the resilience of the human spirit.

2

Chapter 2: Solitude's Embrace

Solitude, often misunderstood, is not merely the absence of company but the presence of oneself. It is a space where one can truly hear their own thoughts and feel their own emotions. In the quiet corners of solitude, we find clarity, reflection, and a profound sense of peace. It is in these moments that we connect with our inner selves, free from the noise and distractions of the world.

While solitude can be daunting, it is also a gateway to self-discovery. It is in the stillness that we confront our true selves, stripped of pretense and facade. Here, we can explore our deepest desires, fears, and aspirations. Solitude allows us to peel back the layers, revealing the core of our being and fostering a deeper understanding of who we are.

However, solitude is not synonymous with loneliness. Loneliness is an ache, a void that yearns for connection, whereas solitude is a choice, a sanctuary for the soul. In solitude, we find the strength to be alone without feeling lonely. It is a testament to our resilience, an acknowledgment that we are complete within ourselves.

Through the embrace of solitude, we cultivate a sense of independence and self-reliance. We learn to cherish our own company and find joy in our own thoughts. In the solitude's embrace, we discover the profound beauty of our own existence, realizing that the journey within is just as significant as the journey without.

3

Chapter 3: Resilient Souls

Resilience is the silent strength that carries us through life's storms. It is the unwavering belief that no matter how fierce the tempest, we have the power to withstand and emerge stronger. It is a testament to the human spirit's capacity to endure, adapt, and thrive in the face of adversity. Resilience is not the absence of struggle but the ability to navigate through it with grace and tenacity.

The path of resilience is often paved with challenges, setbacks, and failures. But it is through these trials that we find our true strength. Each obstacle becomes a stepping stone, teaching us valuable lessons and shaping our character. Resilience is not about never falling; it is about rising each time we fall, with a heart that refuses to give up.

In the face of life's hardships, resilience is the beacon that guides us forward. It is the inner fire that fuels our determination and propels us toward our goals. Resilience is not a trait reserved for the extraordinary; it is a quality inherent in all of us. It is the quiet resolve that whispers, "You can do this," even when the world seems to say otherwise.

As we journey through life, we come to understand that resilience is not about being invincible but about being adaptable. It is the ability to bend without breaking, to find strength in vulnerability, and to turn adversity into opportunity. Resilient souls are those who embrace life's uncertainties with courage and grace, knowing that the human spirit is unbreakable.

Chapter 4: Echoes of Childhood

Childhood is a time of innocence, wonder, and unbridled curiosity. It is a period where the world is a vast playground, and each day is filled with endless possibilities. The echoes of childhood linger in our hearts, reminding us of the carefree days when our spirits were unburdened, and our dreams knew no bounds. It is a chapter of life that shapes our future, leaving an indelible mark on our souls.

As adults, we often find ourselves yearning for the simplicity of our childhood days. The laughter, the adventures, the sense of wonder—all these memories become treasures that we carry with us. Childhood is a reminder of the joy that can be found in the little things, the magic that exists in the world around us. It is a time when our hearts were open, and our minds were free from the constraints of reality.

Yet, childhood is not just about the past; it is also about the lessons we carry forward. It teaches us the importance of play, imagination, and creativity. It reminds us to find joy in the present moment and to approach life with a sense of curiosity and wonder. The echoes of childhood serve as a guide, urging us to reconnect with our inner child and embrace the simple pleasures of life.

In the grand tapestry of life, childhood is a vibrant thread that weaves through our experiences. It is a source of comfort, inspiration, and resilience. By embracing the echoes of our childhood, we honor the journey that brought us here and find the strength to face the future with a heart full of wonder and hope.

5

Chapter 5: The Dance of Solitude and Connection

Life is a delicate dance between solitude and connection. It is in the balance of these two that we find harmony and fulfillment. Solitude allows us to connect with our inner selves, to reflect and grow, while connection brings us closer to others, fostering love, understanding, and empathy. Both are essential, and it is through their interplay that we navigate the complexities of the human experience.

In moments of solitude, we find the space to listen to our own hearts. It is a time for self-care, introspection, and renewal. Solitude is a sanctuary where we can recharge and gain clarity. It is not a retreat from the world but a retreat into ourselves, where we can rediscover our passions, dreams, and values. Through solitude, we cultivate a strong sense of self, which in turn enhances our ability to connect with others.

On the other hand, connection is the lifeblood of human existence. It is through our relationships that we experience love, joy, and a sense of belonging. Connection brings richness to our lives, creating bonds that support and uplift us. It is in the embrace of others that we find comfort, understanding, and shared experiences. Connection reminds us that we are not alone, that our lives are intertwined with those of others.

The dance between solitude and connection is a dynamic one. It requires a delicate balance, an understanding that both are vital to our well-being. By embracing both, we create a life that is both deeply personal and richly communal. We learn to appreciate the beauty of our own company and the joy of shared moments. It is in this dance that we find the true essence of the human soul.

6

Chapter 6: Windows to the Soul

Our eyes are often referred to as windows to the soul, reflecting our innermost thoughts and emotions. They convey what words cannot, revealing the depth of our experiences and the essence of our being. Through the eyes, we connect with others on a profound level, creating a bridge between our inner worlds. The gaze of another can be a powerful force, capable of conveying love, understanding, and empathy.

In moments of true connection, our eyes speak volumes. A glance can convey a lifetime of emotions, from joy and excitement to sorrow and longing. It is through the eyes that we find a sense of intimacy and vulnerability, allowing us to share our deepest selves with others. The eyes are a testament to the complexity of the human experience, a reminder that we are more than the sum of our words and actions.

Yet, the eyes are not just a reflection of our own souls; they are also a mirror to the souls of others. By truly seeing and being seen, we create a space for genuine connection and understanding. In the gaze of another, we find validation, compassion, and a sense of belonging. It is through this mutual exchange that we build bridges of empathy and love.

The eyes, as windows to the soul, remind us of the power of connection. They invite us to look beyond the surface and see the beauty and complexity of the human spirit. Through the eyes, we find a deeper understanding of ourselves and others, realizing that we are all connected in the vast tapestry of life. In this shared gaze, we find the resilience and strength of the human soul.

7

Chapter 7: The Art of Letting Go

Letting go is one of the most challenging yet liberating experiences in life. It requires us to release our grip on the past, allowing ourselves to move forward with grace and acceptance. Letting go is not about forgetting; it is about acknowledging the impact of the past and choosing to embrace the present. It is an act of courage, a testament to our resilience and our ability to adapt to change.

The process of letting go often involves grieving the loss of what once was. It is a journey through sorrow, anger, and ultimately, acceptance. In this process, we learn that it is okay to feel the full spectrum of emotions, to honor our pain, and to give ourselves the time and space to heal. Letting go is a gradual process, a journey that requires patience and self-compassion.

As we let go, we create space for new experiences and opportunities. We allow ourselves to grow and evolve, unburdened by the weight of the past. Letting go is an act of self-love, a recognition that we deserve to move forward with an open heart and an unencumbered spirit. It is a reminder that we are not defined by our past but by our ability to navigate through it with resilience and grace.

Ultimately, letting go is about finding peace within ourselves. It is about accepting that life is a series of transitions and that each ending is a new beginning. By letting go, we honor the journey that brought us here and open ourselves to the endless possibilities that lie ahead. It is through the art of

CHAPTER 7: THE ART OF LETTING GO

letting go that we find the strength to embrace the present and the courage to step into the future.

8

Chapter 8: The Power of Vulnerability

Vulnerability is often perceived as a weakness, but in reality, it is a source of immense strength. It is the courage to be open, to show our true selves, and to embrace the uncertainty of life. Vulnerability is the willingness to be seen, to share our deepest fears and desires, and to connect with others on a profound level. It is through vulnerability that we find true connection and authenticity.

In a world that often values strength and stoicism, embracing vulnerability can be a radical act. It requires us to let go of the need for perfection and to accept ourselves as we are, flaws and all. Vulnerability is not about exposing our weaknesses; it is about acknowledging our humanity and embracing the full range of our emotions. It is through this openness that we find the strength to navigate the complexities of life.

By embracing vulnerability, we create a space for genuine connection and empathy. When we allow ourselves to be vulnerable, we invite others to do the same. It is in this mutual exchange that we build trust, understanding, and compassion. Vulnerability is the foundation of meaningful relationships, a testament to our shared humanity and our ability to support and uplift one another.

Ultimately, vulnerability is a path to resilience and growth. It is through our willingness to be vulnerable that we learn, evolve, and become stronger. By embracing vulnerability, we open ourselves to the richness of life, finding

CHAPTER 8: THE POWER OF VULNERABILITY

beauty in our imperfections and strength in our authenticity. In the embrace of vulnerability, we discover the resilience of the human soul.

9

Chapter 9: The Gift of Presence

In a world that is constantly moving, the gift of presence is a rare and precious treasure. It is the ability to be fully engaged in the moment, to give our undivided attention to the people and experiences that matter most. Presence is a testament to our commitment to living authentically and connecting deeply with ourselves and others. It is a practice that requires mindfulness, intentionality, and a willingness to slow down and savor the present.

Presence is not just about physical proximity; it is about being mentally and emotionally available. It is about truly listening, observing, and engaging with the world around us. When we are present, we create a space for genuine connection and understanding. We honor the people and experiences that enrich our lives, and we cultivate a sense of gratitude for the here and now.

In the practice of presence, we find a deeper sense of fulfillment and peace. By focusing on the present moment, we let go of the worries and distractions that often cloud our minds. We learn to appreciate the beauty of each moment, finding joy in the simple pleasures of life. Presence is a gift that we give to ourselves and others, a reminder that life is happening now, and that every moment is an opportunity for connection and growth.

Ultimately, presence is a practice that strengthens our resilience and enhances our well-being. It is through the gift of presence that we find clarity, purpose, and a deeper sense of connection with ourselves and others.

CHAPTER 9: THE GIFT OF PRESENCE

By embracing the present moment, we honor the journey of life and find the strength to navigate its challenges with grace and authenticity.

10

Chapter 10: The Journey of Self-Discovery

The journey of self-discovery is a lifelong adventure, a quest to uncover the essence of who we are and what truly matters to us. It is a journey that requires curiosity, introspection, and a willingness to explore the depths of our own being. Self-discovery is not about finding a definitive answer but about embracing the ongoing process of growth and transformation.

As we embark on the journey of self-discovery, we encounter various experiences and challenges that shape our identity. Each moment, each decision, and each interaction offers an opportunity to learn more about ourselves. It is through these experiences that we gain insights into our values, passions, and aspirations. The journey of self-discovery is a mosaic of moments, each contributing to the larger picture of who we are.

In the process of self-discovery, we also confront our fears, limitations, and vulnerabilities. It is a journey that requires courage and self-compassion. We learn to embrace our imperfections and to recognize that growth often comes from the challenges we face. Self-discovery is about finding the strength to be true to ourselves, even when it means stepping outside of our comfort zones.

Ultimately, the journey of self-discovery is a path to self-empowerment

CHAPTER 10: THE JOURNEY OF SELF-DISCOVERY

and fulfillment. By understanding ourselves more deeply, we gain the clarity and confidence to pursue our dreams and create a life that is aligned with our values. The journey of self-discovery is an ongoing process, a celebration of the unique and ever-evolving essence of who we are. It is through this journey that we find the resilience and strength to navigate the complexities of life with authenticity and grace.

11

Chapter 11: Finding Beauty in Imperfection

Perfection is an elusive goal, often pursued but rarely attained. In our quest for flawlessness, we often overlook the beauty that lies in imperfection. It is the imperfections that make us unique, that tell the story of our journey and our growth. By embracing our imperfections, we find a deeper sense of authenticity and self-acceptance.

Imperfection is a reminder that we are human, that we are constantly evolving and learning. It is through our mistakes and challenges that we gain wisdom and resilience. Each flaw, each scar, is a testament to our strength and our ability to overcome adversity. By accepting our imperfections, we learn to see them not as weaknesses but as integral parts of our identity.

In the embrace of imperfection, we find freedom from the unrealistic standards of perfection. We learn to appreciate the beauty of our individuality and to celebrate our uniqueness. Imperfection is an invitation to be kind to ourselves, to let go of self-criticism, and to embrace self-compassion. It is a reminder that we are worthy of love and acceptance just as we are.

Ultimately, finding beauty in imperfection is a path to resilience and growth. By accepting and embracing our flaws, we find the strength to be true to ourselves and to navigate life's challenges with grace and authenticity. Imperfection is not a flaw to be hidden but a gift to be celebrated. It is

CHAPTER 11: FINDING BEAUTY IN IMPERFECTION

through our imperfections that we find the true essence of the human soul.

12

Chapter 12: The Strength of Vulnerability

Vulnerability is often perceived as a sign of weakness, but in reality, it is a source of immense strength. It is the courage to be open, to show our true selves, and to embrace the uncertainty of life. Vulnerability is the willingness to be seen, to share our deepest fears and desires, and to connect with others on a profound level. It is through vulnerability that we find true connection and authenticity.

In a world that often values strength and stoicism, embracing vulnerability can be a radical act. It requires us to let go of the need for perfection and to accept ourselves as we are, flaws and all. Vulnerability is not about exposing our weaknesses; it is about acknowledging our humanity and embracing the full range of our emotions. It is through this openness that we find the strength to navigate the complexities of life.

By embracing vulnerability, we create a space for genuine connection and empathy. When we allow ourselves to be vulnerable, we invite others to do the same. It is in this mutual exchange that we build trust, understanding, and compassion. Vulnerability is the foundation of meaningful relationships, a testament to our shared humanity and our ability to support and uplift one another.

Ultimately, vulnerability is a path to resilience and growth. It is through our willingness to be vulnerable that we learn, evolve, and become stronger. By embracing vulnerability, we open ourselves to the richness of life, finding

CHAPTER 12: THE STRENGTH OF VULNERABILITY

beauty in our imperfections and strength in our authenticity. In the embrace of vulnerability, we discover the resilience of the human soul.

13

Chapter 13: The Power of Forgiveness

Forgiveness is a powerful and transformative act, one that liberates both the giver and the receiver. It is the decision to release resentment, anger, and the desire for retribution, choosing instead to embrace compassion, understanding, and healing. Forgiveness is not about condoning wrongdoing but about freeing ourselves from the burden of bitterness and allowing space for growth and reconciliation.

The journey to forgiveness is often a difficult and emotional process. It requires us to confront our pain, to acknowledge the hurt, and to find the strength to let go. Forgiveness is an act of self-compassion, a recognition that holding onto anger only prolongs our suffering. By choosing to forgive, we reclaim our power and create a path to healing and renewal.

In the act of forgiving others, we also find the capacity to forgive ourselves. Self-forgiveness is an essential part of the healing process, allowing us to let go of guilt, shame, and self-judgment. It is a recognition that we are all imperfect beings, capable of making mistakes and learning from them. By forgiving ourselves, we cultivate self-compassion and create a foundation for personal growth and resilience.

Ultimately, forgiveness is an act of strength and courage. It is a testament to our resilience and our ability to transcend pain and adversity. By choosing to forgive, we open our hearts to love, empathy, and understanding. Forgiveness is a powerful force that transforms our relationships and enriches our lives.

CHAPTER 13: THE POWER OF FORGIVENESS

It is through the power of forgiveness that we discover the true essence of the human soul.

14

Chapter 14: The Quest for Meaning

The search for meaning is a fundamental aspect of the human experience. It is the quest to understand our purpose, to find significance in our lives, and to connect with something greater than ourselves. The quest for meaning is a journey of self-discovery, exploration, and introspection. It is a path that leads us to the heart of our existence and the essence of our being.

Meaning is not something that is given to us; it is something that we create through our choices, actions, and relationships. It is found in the pursuit of our passions, the connections we build, and the impact we have on the world. The quest for meaning is an ongoing process, a journey that evolves as we grow and change. It is through this quest that we find a sense of purpose and fulfillment.

In the search for meaning, we also encounter moments of doubt, uncertainty, and existential questioning. These moments are an integral part of the journey, challenging us to dig deeper and to seek answers within ourselves. It is through these challenges that we gain a deeper understanding of our values, beliefs, and aspirations. The quest for meaning is a journey of resilience, requiring us to navigate the complexities of life with courage and perseverance.

Ultimately, the quest for meaning is a path to self-empowerment and enlightenment. By seeking and creating meaning in our lives, we find the strength to face adversity, the clarity to pursue our dreams, and the wisdom to live authentically. The quest for meaning is a celebration of the human spirit, a testament to our resilience and our ability to find purpose and joy in the journey of life.

15

Chapter 15: Embracing Change

Change is a constant in life, an inevitable force that shapes our experiences and our growth. It is often met with resistance and fear, yet it is through change that we find opportunities for transformation and renewal. Embracing change requires us to let go of the familiar and to open ourselves to the unknown. It is a testament to our resilience and our ability to adapt to new circumstances.

The process of embracing change often involves a period of transition, where we navigate the uncertainty and challenges that come with it. It is a journey that requires courage, flexibility, and a willingness to learn. By embracing change, we find the strength to move forward and to create new paths for ourselves. Change is not something to be feared; it is an opportunity for growth and self-discovery.

In the embrace of change, we also find the power to reinvent ourselves. Each change brings a chance to start anew, to redefine our goals, and to pursue our dreams with renewed vigor. It is through change that we find the resilience to overcome obstacles and to transform our lives. Embracing change is an act of self-empowerment, a recognition that we have the ability to shape our own destiny.

Ultimately, change is a force that propels us forward, guiding us on the journey of life. By embracing change, we find the strength to navigate its complexities and the wisdom to appreciate its opportunities. Change is a reminder that life is dynamic and ever-evolving, and that each moment is an opportunity for growth and renewal. It is through the embrace of change that we discover the resilience of the human soul.

16

Chapter 16: The Language of Silence

Silence is a powerful and often overlooked aspect of communication. It is the space between words, the pause that allows us to reflect and connect on a deeper level. The language of silence is one that transcends words, conveying emotions, thoughts, and intentions in a profound way. It is through silence that we find clarity, understanding, and a sense of peace.

In moments of silence, we create a space for introspection and self-awareness. Silence allows us to listen to our own thoughts and to connect with our inner selves. It is a sanctuary where we can process our emotions and gain insights into our experiences. The language of silence is one of self-discovery, a reminder that sometimes the most powerful communication is found in the absence of words.

Silence also plays a crucial role in our relationships with others. It is in the quiet moments that we find true connection and understanding. By embracing silence, we create a space for empathy and compassion, allowing us to listen and be present with others. The language of silence is a testament to the power of non-verbal communication, a reminder that sometimes the most meaningful exchanges happen without words.

Ultimately, silence is a tool for resilience and growth. It is through silence that we find the strength to navigate life's challenges and the wisdom to appreciate its moments of stillness. The language of silence is a celebration of

CHAPTER 16: THE LANGUAGE OF SILENCE

the human spirit, a recognition that we are more than our words and actions. In the embrace of silence, we discover the true essence of the human soul.

17

Chapter 17: The Resilience of Love

Love is the cornerstone of the human experience, a force that transcends time and space. It is through love that we find connection, joy, and a sense of belonging. Love is resilient, enduring through life's challenges and growing stronger with each passing day. It is a testament to the strength of the human soul and its capacity to give and receive love.

The journey of love is often filled with moments of joy and sorrow, growth and learning. It is a path that requires vulnerability, trust, and a willingness to embrace both the highs and lows. Love is not just a feeling; it is an action, a commitment to support, uplift, and cherish one another. It is through love that we find the strength to face adversity and the courage to pursue our dreams.

Love also plays a crucial role in our self-discovery and personal growth. It is through love that we learn to see ourselves through the eyes of others, finding acceptance and compassion. Love teaches us the importance of empathy, understanding, and forgiveness. It is a source of resilience, guiding us through life's challenges with grace and hope.

Ultimately, love is the foundation of our resilience and the essence of our humanity. It is through love that we find the strength to navigate life's complexities and the wisdom to appreciate its beauty. The resilience of love is a celebration of the human spirit, a recognition that we are all connected in the vast tapestry of life. In the embrace of love, we discover the true essence of the human soul.

Curious Hearts: Exploring Nostalgia, Solitude, and the Resilience of the Human Soul

"Curious Hearts" is a heartfelt exploration of the intricate tapestry of human emotions and experiences. Through the lens of nostalgia, solitude, and resilience, this book delves into the profound aspects of the human soul. Each chapter invites readers to embark on a journey of self-discovery, reflection, and growth.

Nostalgia, with its bittersweet embrace, reminds us of the cherished moments of the past and their enduring impact on our present lives. Solitude, often misunderstood, is celebrated as a space for introspection and inner peace. Resilience, the silent strength within us, shines through as a testament to our ability to navigate life's challenges with grace and determination.

"Curious Hearts" is a tribute to the beauty of imperfection, the power of vulnerability, and the transformative nature of forgiveness and love. It encourages readers to embrace change, find meaning in their journey, and appreciate the profound connection between silence and communication.

Through vivid storytelling and thoughtful reflection, "Curious Hearts" illuminates the resilience of the human spirit and the richness of the human experience. It is a celebration of life's complexities and a reminder of the strength and beauty that reside within each of us.

www.ingramcontent.com/pod-product-compliance
Lightning Source LLC
LaVergne TN
LVHW010443070526
838199LV00066B/6165